You Are There!

San Francisco 1906

Kenneth C. H. Walsh

Consultants

Timothy Rasinski, Ph.D.
Kent State University

Lori Oczkus, M.A.
Literacy Consultant

Publishing Credits

Rachelle Cracchiolo, M.S.Ed., *Publisher*
Conni Medina, M.A.Ed., *Managing Editor*
Dona Herweck Rice, *Series Developer*
Emily R. Smith, M.A.Ed., *Content Director*
Stephanie Bernard/Susan Daddis, M.A.Ed., *Editors*
Robin Erickson, *Senior Graphic Designer*

The TIME logo is a registered trademark of TIME Inc.
Used under license.

Image Credits: Cover and p.1 Look and Learn/Bridgeman Images;
pp.2–3 Bettmann/Getty Images; pp.4–5 PhotoQuest/Getty Images;
pp.6–7 Spencer Weiner/Los Angeles Times via Getty Images; pp.8–9,
14–15 Science Source; pp.16–17 Buyenlarge/Getty Images; pp.18–19
World History Archive/Alamy Stock Photo; pp.20–21 PF-(usna)/Alamy
Stock Photo; pp.22–23 Everett Collection Historical/Alamy Stock
Photo; pp.24–25 Chronicle/Alamy Stock Photo; pp.26–27 Lebrecht
Music and Arts Photo Library/Alamy Stock Photo; all other images
from iStock and/or Shutterstock.

Library of Congress Cataloging-in-Publication Data

Names: Walsh, Kenneth C. H., author.
Title: You are there! San Francisco 1906 / Kenneth C. H. Walsh.
Description: Huntington Beach, CA : Teacher Created Materials, [2017] |
  Includes index. | Audience: Grades 7-8.
Identifiers: LCCN 2016035000 (print) | LCCN 2016035341 (ebook) | ISBN
  9781493836178 (pbk.) | ISBN 9781480757219 (eBook)
Subjects: LCSH: San Francisco Earthquake and Fire, Calif.,
1906--Juvenile
  literature. | Earthquakes--California--San Francisco--History--20th
  century--Juvenile literature. | Fires--California--San
  Francisco--History--20th century--Juvenile literature. | San Francisco
  (Calif.)--History--20th century--Juvenile literature.
Classification: LCC F869.S357 W35 2017 (print) | LCC F869.S357 (ebook)
| DDC
  979.4/61051--dc23
LC record available at https://lccn.loc.gov/2016035000

Teacher Created Materials

5301 Oceanus Drive
Huntington Beach, CA 92649-1030
http://www.tcmpub.com

ISBN 978-1-4938-3617-8

© 2017 Teacher Created Materials, Inc.

Table of Contents

Goodnight, San Francisco

It's another beautiful San Francisco sunset. Under the shades of pink and gold, dockworkers, shopkeepers, and business people head home. It is the evening of April 17, 1906. It has been a day like any other for the citizens of the city. San Francisco is alive and buzzing.

The city has grown immensely over the last 60 years. With a population of over 400,000 people, it is the ninth-largest city in the United States. Following the California Gold Rush, San Francisco is the economic center of the West Coast. The bustling city is located right on a bay. Because of this prime location, San Francisco is the busiest port in the region, and it is here that countless ships are loaded and sent all around the world. The city is even referred to as the "gateway to the Pacific" because of its links to the rest of the world.

Unstable Ground

San Francisco sits on the San Andreas **Fault.** This is a strike-slip fault, where the Pacific Plate moves northwest relative to its neighbor, the North American Plate. The San Andreas Fault is among the most active fault lines in the world, and earthquakes along it are common.

Gold Rush Boom

In January 1848, gold was discovered in the Sacramento Valley. About 20,000 people flocked to San Francisco in hopes of finding gold. By the end of 1849, 100,000 more people moved to California to make their fortunes.

Market Street before the earthquake

Due to its global connections, San Francisco is also the **cultural** hub of the western United States. Similar to port cities on the East Coast, San Francisco is influenced by a wide array of immigrants settling in the city. There is interaction among people of all nationalities and backgrounds.

Aside from its position as a center of trade and culture, San Francisco is also an important part of the United States military. Its ports give the military a base of operations with access to Asia and many other territories in the Pacific Ocean.

miners during the early years of the California Gold Rush

Until this point, nothing seems to stand in the way of San Francisco's rise. It is among the largest cities in the United States. It is prosperous and vibrant. But when night falls on this April day, an unexpected shift is stirring. With the new dawn, the landscape is in danger of being changed forever. Will the city be able to withstand the earth-rattling events to come?

Shake Up!

In the decades leading up to the 1906 earthquake, there had been an increase in **seismic** activity in the San Francisco area.

THINK LINK

◎ For what reason might building a major city near a fault line be worth the risks?

◎ In what ways might the people of San Francisco have prepared for a major earthquake?

◎ Why do you think people choose to live somewhere that is prone to earthquake activity or other natural disasters?

A Morning Jolt!

BOOM! The citizens of San Francisco rise from their beds as a shock hits the city. It is 5:12 on the morning of April 18, 1906. Some local workers have begun their days, but the sun isn't up yet. As seconds pass quietly, the shaking slows, and everything seems fine. This region has experienced increased earthquake activity in recent years, so this isn't too alarming.

Another boom! This time, the shock lasts 45 seconds. Any residents who weren't awakened by the initial shock are certainly disturbed now. The **tectonic plates** of Earth's surface shake with violent fury as people scramble for safety wherever they can find it. The city rattles for what seems like an eternity, and buildings across San Francisco begin to crumble as the **tremors** continue. The big earthquake has hit.

A Wide Radius

The 1906 earthquake affected about 375,000 square miles (971,000 square kilometers). About half of that area was in the Pacific Ocean.

Careful Construction

At the time of the earthquake, buildings were not made with the same safety measures they are built with today. Structures were not designed to withstand the intense shaking that occurred. Consequently, the damage was massive.

Chinatown after the earthquake

People of the city are left reeling by the severity of the quake. The **reverberations** are felt all over the surrounding regions. Cities such as San Jose and Santa Rosa suffer major damage, fires, and loss of life. The actual **epicenter** of the quake is offshore in the Pacific Ocean, but the closest point to the epicenter is most likely Mussel Rock. This rock formation is located just offshore of the San Francisco suburbs. The oceanic epicenter causes a **tsunami**, which is registered at the nearby San Francisco **Presidio**.

In a matter of minutes, San Francisco is reduced to a pile of rubble. Just hours before, a bright and vibrant metropolis buzzed with activity. Now, the city is silent. The people are stunned.

Unfortunately, this is only the beginning. More challenges lie ahead for the city and the people of San Francisco.

PACIFIC

Off the Charts

Although the **Richter magnitude scale** would not be invented for a few decades, the 1906 earthquake is estimated to have registered at 7.8. The quake was also classified from VII to IX on the Modified Mercalli Intensity (MMI) scale and a 9 on a scale of 1 to 10 on the Rossi Forel Scale.

OCEAN

Key

★ capital

── San Andreas Fault line

◎ epicenter

Nevada

Goose Lake

Klamath R.

Clair Engle L.

Shasta L.

Eagle L.

Honey L.

Eel R.

Russian R.

Clear L.

Sacramento R.

Feather R.

Lake Tahoe

★ **SACRAMENTO**

Santa Rosa •

Vallejo •

• Concord

Oakland

• Stockton

Molelumne R.

Stanislaus R.

Yosemite N. Park

Mono Lake

San Francisco •

Daly City

• Hayward

Fremont

• San Jose

• Modesto

Merced R.

• Merced

Kings Canyon National Park

Owens R.

Monterey Bay

• Salinas

San Joaquin R.

• Fresno

Sequoia N. P.

Owens Lake

Pinnacles N. P.

Salinas R.

• Visalia

• Porterville

• Delano

Kern R.

• Bakersfield

Buena Vista L.

Los Angeles •

STOP! THINK...

◎ How far from San Francisco could the shaking be felt?

◎ What other cities were in the high-intensity zone?

◎ What kind of impact may have been felt in Los Angeles?

San Diego •

A Look Below the Surface

There are three different types of faults in Earth's crust: normal, reverse (thrust), and strike-slip. They are categorized by how the tectonic plates move in relation to one another. The San Andreas Fault is a strike-slip, which means that the two plates slide past each other without rising or falling. This is what happened in the San Francisco earthquake of 1906. Take a look at this diagram to understand the anatomy of an earthquake.

footwall

hanging wall

Strike-slip: The plates move sideways next to each other. The key distinction is that neither plate is moving up or down.

hanging wall

footwall

Reverse (thrust): The hanging wall rises relative to the **footwall**.

Normal: The **hanging wall** drops relative to the footwall.

footwall

hanging wall

Buildings Fall, Flames Rise

Over the next four days, several fires ravage the city. Flames devour what the earthquake has left behind. The movement of the ground during the earthquake has compromised the safety of the city. Water and gas are distributed to customers from their source points (for example, power plants) through a series of large pipes called **mains**. Above ground, downed power lines spark fires. Below ground, gas and water mains are easily broken.

Devastating Damage

More than 25,000 buildings are burned during the disaster, and the damage spans nearly 500 city blocks and 2,800 acres. In the end, about 90 percent of the destruction will actually be caused by fires, not the earthquake.

The leaked gas explodes and ignites. Severed water mains cut off firefighters' access to water to combat the flames. Buildings do not have the structural **integrities** to stand. They also do not have protections against the spread of fires. The city is unprepared for this disaster. San Francisco is an **inferno**.

296 Miles

The rupture along the San Andreas Fault during the 1906 earthquake was 296 miles (476 kilometers) long. In 1989, another high magnitude earthquake hit the city. This one only had a rupture length of 25 miles (40 kilometers). This means that the 1906 earthquake had about 30 times more energy and power than the 1989 quake.

Fire Department Troubles

Dennis T. Sullivan is the San Francisco fire chief. He is gravely injured during the earthquake. In fact, Sullivan's injuries appear life-threatening. He is unable to lead the fight against the fire. The fire department is ill-prepared to handle his sudden absence. They struggle to overcome the blazes.

The San Francisco Fire Department sends a request to the Presidio for dynamite. The Presidio is an army base in San Francisco. The army is a huge help and support for the city during the crisis. They supply the fire department with the requested explosives.

The dynamite is to be used to create **firebreaks** to contain and control the flames. However, the plan doesn't work. The use of dynamite by firefighters and soldiers, who are not properly trained to work with the explosives, actually causes more fires. Numerous buildings are set ablaze unintentionally. The situation quickly escalates from bad to worse.

Kaboom!

Dynamite has many uses. While it backfired in San Francisco, dynamite can be very helpful in construction and demolition.

Quick Replacement

Dennis T. Sullivan died from the injuries he suffered during the earthquake. Frederick Funston, a U.S. army general who had no training or experience fighting fires, took over leadership of the city after Sullivan passed away.

firefighters battling the flames in San Francisco

Other fires around the city start more conventionally. One of the largest fires breaks out at 395 Hayes Street. It originates in a home kitchen, where a woman is making breakfast for her family. People would one day call it the "Ham and Eggs Fire."

However, not every fire is accidental. As the city lies in ruins, the citizens of San Francisco do the unthinkable and begin to intentionally burn some buildings that have been damaged in the earthquake. Insurance policies in the area tend to offer coverage for fire damage but not damage from earthquakes. To ensure **compensation** for their losses, residents set fire to their own homes and businesses.

Ham and Eggs Fire

The residents at 395 Hayes Street didn't know the chimney of their stove was damaged in the earthquake. When they began to cook breakfast, it caused the whole kitchen to ignite. Firefighters arrived quickly, but the earthquake had cut off necessary water supplies. So, the firefighters were helpless.

Without considering the dangerous consequences, people are actively contributing to the massive damage. The city is on the brink of utter destruction. Who will help? Will help arrive before it's too late?

Mass Exodus

In the aftermath of the earthquake, people could be seen dragging suitcases and trunks with their belongings to parks and other open areas. Areas such as Golden Gate Park became full of people looking for safety.

the scene on Sacramento Street after the earthquake

Welcome Relief

In the days following the earthquake, help arrives for San Francisco. The United States military steps in to provide services for the city and its citizens. More than 4,000 American soldiers serve in the relief efforts. They patrol the streets and guard important government buildings. They help stop looters from ransacking the city.

a military camp, days after the earthquake

Help, Don't Hurt

Sadly, some members of the military who assisted in the relief efforts of the disaster abandoned their commands. There were multiple reports of soldiers who participated in the **looting**. Thankfully, the overwhelming majority of soldiers followed their orders and aided the recovery efforts.

In addition, the army begins to build **relief houses** to shelter those in need. There are about 5,600 houses grouped in camps throughout San Francisco. The houses are stacked very close together to maximize space. When completed, the houses will be rented out to the **displaced** citizens. It may not be home, but having shelter is a big relief.

Red Cross

The American Red Cross provides aid in times of emergency. Its founder, Clara Barton, had left the organization two years before the 1906 quake. The relief group was still reforming, but eventually, the Red Cross was able to provide food kitchens, grants for rebuilding, and the construction of some housing for San Franciscans.

All city residents are allotted daily meals at various soup kitchens around the city. In addition, people from neighboring states send provisions such as bread and **produce**. These supplies come from as far away as Utah and Idaho.

Help doesn't only come from inside the country. People around the world send donations and other aid to the citizens of San Francisco. After only a few days, the donations total over $5 million. Other nations, businesses, and even wealthy individuals contribute to the cause. The United States government donates $1 million of relief supplies. These include food for the soup kitchens and tents for sheltering the displaced victims.

The earthquake and subsequent fires are a terrible disaster. They leave the city of San Francisco in ruins. But the city won't stay down for long. The citizens are strong. With the help of people from both America and around the globe, San Francisco will recover.

Photo Evidence

In the 1870s, **photojournalism** became an active enterprise. But the San Francisco earthquake of 1906 marked the first natural disaster in history to be covered photographically. Through photographs, the disaster became "real" for people everywhere. That may be one reason why there was such an outpouring of financial support.

Outpouring of Support

Donations for San Francisco's recovery came from many different sources. The Standard Oil Company gave $100,000 and so did businessman Andrew Carnegie.

Red Cross workers feeding people left homeless after the earthquake

What's Left?

The San Francisco earthquake of 1906 will live in **infamy**. The most devastating loss is the number of people killed. Over 3,000 people die in the tragedy. This is the highest death toll for a natural disaster in the history of California.

The area surrounding San Francisco is likely changed forever. The mouth of the Salinas River used to empty into Monterey Bay. Now, it is redirected farther south. The shifting of the tectonic plates has **diverted** the flow of water.

Over 80 percent of San Francisco is destroyed. Very little is left of the sprawling metropolis that stood just a few days prior. More than half of San Francisco's 400,000 residents are displaced. Many of the homeless people have no choice but to settle in **refugee camps** and will likely have to stay there for quite some time.

The earthquake and fires will be remembered as one of the worst natural disasters in world history.

Avoiding Another Disaster

There was great pressure to rebuild San Francisco quickly. Many people wanted to use the abundant local redwood forests for **reconstruction**. To protect the long-standing trees, the Muir Woods National Monument was eventually formed.

A High Cost

The total cost of damages caused by the earthquake and the fires was $400 million. That's equivalent to about $10 billion today.

The Road to Recovery

The year is 1915. The Panama-Pacific International Exposition world fair is being held in San Francisco. It is meant to celebrate the completion of the Panama Canal. But it also serves as an opportunity to showcase and celebrate the city's incredible reconstruction.

In the nine years since the earthquake, the city has been steadily rebuilt. Restoration plans began immediately after the disaster. The destroyed city was reborn after much hard work.

In the wake of San Francisco's destruction, commerce and people moved south to Los Angeles. That city has now become the hub of trade and business in the West.

Every year since the earthquake, the city of San Francisco **commemorates** the disaster. The remaining survivors gather at 5:12 a.m. each April 18. They remember the horrors of 1906, but they also celebrate the lives they lead today and the strength of the city.

83 Years Later

An earthquake measuring 6.9 on the Richter scale struck San Francisco on October 17, 1989. It hit at about 5:00 p.m., just before the start of the third game of Major League Baseball's World Series. The game was between the San Francisco Giants and the Oakland Athletics. The quake caused the series to be delayed for 10 days.

Lotta's Fountain

In the years following the earthquake, survivors would meet at Lotta's Fountain on Market Street in the Financial District. They would exchange goods, services, or information. Today, city officials and citizens still meet every April 18 at the fountain to remember the disaster and the people who were lost.

Glossary

commemorates—ceremony to honor and remember an event or people

compensation—something that is given, usually money, in case of loss, injury, or death

cultural—qualities in a society or group of people that come from their habits, beliefs, traditions, art, etc.

displaced—without a home

diverted—changed the direction of something

epicenter—the part of Earth's surface directly above where an earthquake originates

fault—a break in Earth's crust

firebreaks—areas of land that have been cleared to stop the spread of fires

footwall—a block of rock located below a slanted fault

hanging wall—a block of rock lying above a slanted fault

infamy—being known for a bad reason

inferno—a hot, fiery place

integrities—structural frameworks in perfect condition

looting—stealing things after destruction has been caused by disaster, fire, rioting, etc.

mains—the largest pipe in a system of connected pipes

photojournalism—using photographs to report news stories

Presidio—an army post

produce—fruits and vegetables

reconstruction—rebuilding of an area after a disaster

refugee camps—temporary settlements built to provide shelter for displaced victims

relief houses—shelters built for displaced victims

reverberations—continuing effects or repercussions

Richter magnitude scale—assigns a magnitude number to quantify the energy released by an earthquake

seismic—relating to the vibration of the earth, either by man-made or natural causes

tectonic plates—the two sub-layers of Earth's crust that move and sometimes fracture, causing earthquakes

tremors—involuntary shaking of the ground before, during, and/or after earthquakes

tsunami—a high, large ocean wave usually caused by an earthquake

Index

Check It Out!

Books

Gregory, Kristiana. 2003. *Earthquake at Dawn*. Demco Media.

Kurzman, Dan. 2002. *Disaster! The Great San Francisco Earthquake and Fire of 1906*. G.K. Hall.

Lee, Stacey. 2016. *Outrun the Moon*. G. P. Putnam's Sons Books for Young Readers.

Madonia, Kristen-Paige. 2016. *Invisible Fault Lines*. Simon & Schuster Books for Young Readers.

Videos

Weidlinger, Tom. *American Experience: The Great San Francisco Earthquake*. PBS.

Websites

Exploratorium. *Faultline: Seismic Science at the Epicenter*. http://www.exploratorium.edu/faultline/index.html.

Library of Congress. *San Francisco Earthquake and Fire, April 18, 1906*. https://www.loc.gov/item/00694425.

National Archives. *San Francisco Earthquake, 1906*. https://www.archives.gov/legislative/features/sf/.

Try It!

Imagine you are one of the architects brought in after the earthquake and fires to help rebuild San Francisco.

- Are you going to help reconstruct in a residential area or a business area?

- What materials will you use knowing what you've learned from the 1906 earthquake? Will you make special considerations for plumbing, gas, and electrical lines? Use information and photographs from this reader as well as other resources.

- Sketch a dwelling or business you would like to see rebuilt in the city.

- Label all materials and special features you want to include to make this structure better able to withstand a strong earthquake and the aftermath.

- Write a paragraph including how you developed your structure and why you think it would work in an earthquake-prone area.

About the Author

Kenneth C. H. Walsh is a California native and has lived through many earthquakes—but nothing like the San Francisco earthquake in 1906! He likes to spend time under the California sun with his girlfriend, friends, and family—especially his younger brother. Kenneth is an avid sports fan, and he especially enjoys basketball and soccer. He also likes listening to music, playing video games, and eating! His favorite foods are pasta, sushi, and breakfast burritos. Kenneth is pursuing a career in the sports industry.